GUIL

MW01114682

Family
Ministries

*Supporting Families
for Faith and
Service*

MaryJane Pierce Norton
General Board of Discipleship

FAMILY MINISTRIES

Copyright © 2012 by Cokesbury

ISBN 978-1-426-73668-1

Some paragraph numbers for and language in the Book of Discipline *may have changed in the 2012 revision, which was published after these Guidelines were printed. We regret any inconvenience.*

Contents

Called to a Ministry of Faithfulness and Vitality 4

Called to Lead Family Ministries 6

    A Biblical Foundation

    Affirmation for Families

    Preparing for Your Ministry

Guidance for the Leader in Family Ministries 11

    Prayer and Spiritual Guidance

    Knowing the Families We Seek to Serve

    Advocate for Families

Leading the Team 15

    The Family Ministries Team Meetings

    Planning for Ministry

Evaluation of Family Ministries 23

    What Results Do You Want?

Family Ministry Models 25

    A Flexible "Family" Concept

Calendar for Family Ministries 28

Resources 31

General Agency Contacts   **Inside Back Cover**

Called to a Ministry of Faithfulness and Vitality

You are so important to the life of the Christian church! You have consented to join with other people of faith who, through the millennia, have sustained the church by extending God's love to others. You have been called and have committed your unique passions, gifts, and abilities to a position of leadership. This Guideline will help you understand the basic elements of that ministry within your own church and within The United Methodist Church.

Leadership in Vital Ministry

Each person is called to ministry by virtue of his or her baptism, and that ministry takes place in all aspects of daily life, both in and outside of the church. Your leadership role requires that you will be a faithful participant in the **mission of the church**, which is to partner with God to **make disciples of Jesus Christ for the transformation of the world**. You will not only engage in your area of ministry, but will also work to empower others to be in ministry as well. The vitality of your church, and the Church as a whole, depends upon the faith, abilities, and actions of all who work together for the glory of God.

Clearly then, as a pastoral leader or leader among the laity, your ministry is not just a "job," but a spiritual endeavor. You are a spiritual leader now, and others will look to you for spiritual leadership. What does this mean?

All persons who follow Jesus are called to grow spiritually through the practice of various Christian habits (or "means of grace") such as prayer, Bible study, private and corporate worship, acts of service, Christian conferencing, and so on. Jesus taught his disciples practices of spiritual growth and leadership that you will model as you guide others. As members of the congregation grow through the means of grace, they will assume their own role in ministry and help others in the same way. This is the cycle of disciple making.

The Church's Vision

While there is one mission—to make disciples of Jesus Christ—the portrait of a successful mission will differ from one congregation to the next. One of your roles is to listen deeply for the guidance and call of God in your own context. In your church, neighborhood, or greater community, what are the greatest needs? How is God calling your congregation to be in a ministry of service and witness where they are? What does vital ministry look like in the life of your congregation and its neighbors? What are the characteristics, traits, and actions that identify a person as a faithful disciple in your context?

This portrait, or vision, is formed when you and the other leaders discern together how your gifts from God come together to fulfill the will of God.

Assessing Your Efforts

We are generally good at deciding what to do, but we sometimes skip the more important first question of what we want to accomplish. Knowing your task (the mission of disciple making) and knowing what results you want (the vision of your church) are the first two steps in a vital ministry. The third step is in knowing how you will assess or measure the results of what you do and who you are (and become) because of what you do. Those measures relate directly to mission and vision, and they are more than just numbers.

One of your leadership tasks will be to take a hard look, with your team, at all the things your ministry area does or plans to do. No doubt they are good and worthy activities; the question is, *"Do these activities and experiences lead people into a mature relationship with God and a life of deeper discipleship?"* That is the business of the church, and the church needs to do what only the church can do. You may need to eliminate or alter some of what you do if it does not measure up to the standard of faithful disciple making. It will be up to your ministry team to establish the specific standards against which you compare all that you do and hope to do. (This Guideline includes further help in establishing goals, strategies, and measures for this area of ministry.)

The Mission of The United Methodist Church

Each local church is unique, yet it is a part of a *connection,* a living organism of the body of Christ. Being a connectional Church means in part that all United Methodist churches are interrelated through the structure and organization of districts, conferences, and jurisdictions in the larger "family" of the denomination. *The Book of Discipline of The United Methodist Church* describes, among other things, the ministry of all United Methodist Christians, the essence of servant ministry and leadership, how to organize and accomplish that ministry, and how our connectional structure works (see especially ¶¶126–138).

Our Church extends way beyond your doorstep; it is a global Church with both local and international presence. You are not alone. The resources of the entire denomination are intended to assist you in ministry. With this help and the partnership of God and one another, the mission continues. You are an integral part of God's church and God's plan!

(For help in addition to this Guideline and the *Book of Discipline*, see "Resources" at the end of your Guideline, www.umc.org, and the other websites listed on the inside back cover.)

Called to Lead Family Ministries

Y ou have been selected to lead family ministries in your congregation. This call should fill you with hope as you find ways for God's love to be shared in homes in your congregation and community. As you read this Guideline, keep in mind what is meant by "family ministry." It is much more than planning a yearly meal for the whole congregation. Family ministry is ministry by, with, and for families. Some might say that family ministry is all that the church does, and because it embraces every age and stage of life, that would be true. Think of it in this way: Family ministry is identifying and enabling all to see Christ-like relationship qualities among those who call one another "family"; equipping households to be centers of faith; providing to those households of faith opportunities for mission and service; and attracting others to be part of the congregation because of their actions. Family ministry extends the table of fellowship to not just those within the church congregation, but to those who stand outside, welcoming them in to live in the community of the family of God.

As the designated leader for family ministries in your congregation you will:
• work with the other leaders in your congregation to plan and implement ministry in order to fulfill the church's mission of helping all persons become disciples of Jesus Christ for the transformation of the world
• address the needs of families in your church and community so that all may grow in the Christian faith and live both at home and at church as disciples of Jesus Christ

I would invite you to enter into a time of prayer as you begin your task.
O God of all families, help me as I lead my congregation to be open to the many possibilities for family ministries within our congregation. Help me lead our congregation so that it can be an open door through which all families can come to know you. Help me work in such a way that my ego and my needs do not shape our ministries for families. Open my mind and those who will work in family ministries so that we can see all the needs of families, but do not let us be paralyzed by those needs. Let hospitality, graciousness, love, and kindness be our guide as we plan and work on behalf of families in our congregation and in our community. Amen.

A Biblical Foundation
God has entrusted tremendous power to human relationships. In the Scriptures we see story after story of families. Think of the witness of Abraham and Sarah; or Ruth, Naomi, and Boaz; or Mary, Martha, and

Lazarus; or Timothy, Lois, and Eunice. (See, for example, Genesis 18; Ruth 1–4; John 11:1-44; 2 Timothy 1:3-7.) Take a minute and think of the stories of biblical families that you remember. Make notes about what is seen regarding families and relationships in each of these stories.

Through these stories of biblical families we see God's interest in human relationship and God's purpose carried out sometimes through and sometimes in spite of those relationships. We are called as God's people, living in relation to others, to be loving and just, enabling one another to grow in faith.

We receive images of practices within the family and in the home that form the faith experiences of children, youth, and adults. These reflect the life of the worshipping community, the ordinary and extra-ordinary times in the family. Through Scripture we see:

- The reminder that we are to love God, keep God's commandments, recite them to our children, and remember them as we rise and as we lie down. (See Deuteronomy 6.)

- Mary and Joseph bringing their infant son to the Temple, where they are greeted by Anna and Simeon, who proclaim God's plans for their young son. (See Luke 2.)

- Timothy learning about faith from both his grandmother Lois and his mother Eunice. (See 2 Timothy 1.)

- Paul's teaching to remember the stranger and extend hospitality and care. (See, for example, Galatians 6.)

Support for living faithfully day-by-day and lifting up the best ways to live in relationship with one another is part of family ministry. Unfortunately, because we are human, the relationships with those closest to us are often broken by such simple things as lack of time, poor communication, and self-centeredness or by such complex issues as abuse. Thus, family ministry addresses the brokenness that occurs in families and seeks to build support for regaining health in human relationships. There is need in the family—as well as in the congregation—to proclaim and hear the good news.

AN AFFIRMATION FOR FAMILIES

This Guideline is designed to direct, motivate, and assist you. What follows is a brief description of your tasks. After this job description, you will find further information for performing the tasks laid out. Finally, there are models for ministry that may be helpful to you in your situation. Consider first the Affirmation for Families on page 8.

Affirmation for Families

We believe that the family is the primary community through which persons enter into life. Entry is made by diverse means among which are birth, adoption, and covenant. Through this primary community, persons are received in love and given their identity and self-worth. Persons are nurtured and guided in their growth and understanding of their spiritual and cultural heritages. They are encouraged to seek their vocation as children of God.

We believe that families are communities of commitment that are diverse in size, configuration, ethnicity, and culture. We believe these families have strengths and gifts that should be affirmed, celebrated, and supported. We believe that where families are is where the church needs to be.

We believe the mission of the family is human growth and faith development. Each family is charged with the responsibility to provide the environment, resources, and support that enable individual members to reach their optimal level of growth and development in every dimension of life. In the Christian tradition, spiritual development and values formation are an intentional part of the family missional task.

We believe that families have a responsibility to live daily lives of faithful discipleship.

We believe in the shared responsibility of parenting by men and women who are responsible for children in the household.

We believe children and youth are to be shown and taught the meaning of the Christian faith and the observance of the disciplines of the faith.

We believe that the local congregation is the faith community into which diverse families are received, assisted in their faith development and spiritual growth, guided and equipped for ministry, and supported as they live out their faith daily in the community and the world. Through their ministries, congregations are intentional in developing and improving systems that enable and support the quality of life for families.

Preparing for Your Ministry

Take time for a thoughtful beginning, before you are caught up in all the activity of the different classes, groups, and events.

Pray for the families in your congregation and in your community. Begin your job as a leader in family ministry by intentionally praying for the families you currently serve and those you seek to serve through the ministries of your congregation. You will be a spiritual leader for your congregation in family ministries.

Collect information on the families in your congregation and the families you seek to serve in your community. You will be one of the primary sources of information about families to other leaders in your congregation. Use surveys, personal interviews, and resource materials to study the needs of families in your congregation and your community.

Analyze how your congregation is serving families in light of the mission and the process for carrying out our mission. The *Book of Discipline* states that "the local church provides the most significant arena through which disciple-making occurs" (¶201). Furthermore, the function of the local church is described:

"The function of the local church, under the guidance of the Holy Spirit, is to help people to accept and confess Jesus Christ as Lord and Savior and to live their daily lives in light of their relationship with God. Therefore, the local church is to minister to persons in the community where the church is located, to provide appropriate training and nurture to all, to cooperate in ministry with other local churches, to defend God's creation and live as an ecologically responsible community, and to participate in the worldwide mission of the church, as minimal expectations of an authentic church" (¶202).

Begin by asking these questions:

- How do the family ministries in my congregation support making disciples of Jesus Christ for the transformation of the world?

- How effectively do we reach out to persons and relate them to God? How well do we nurture persons in the faith and send them forth as servants of Christ?

- Look at what you are currently doing. What are the needs of the families in your congregation? Where are the gaps in what they need as it relates to fulfilling the mission of the church?

Communicate with other leaders in the congregation to let those leaders know the needs of families. Ask each leader to plan in his or her area (such as Christian education, stewardship, evangelism, and worship), keeping in mind the needs of the families you serve in your congregation and community.

Participate in church council and other meetings as needed. Consider your attendance as an important part of your job. As you listen and participate in these meetings, use this as a forum to state the needs of families and ask for these needs to be addressed as plans are made for ministry.

Organize a group of people to help you in planning and leading the congregation in family ministry. In some congregations, this group is chosen for you by the committee on lay leadership. In others, the leader must recruit a group of people. Choose those in your congregation who have a passion, knowledge, and skills in various areas of family ministry. For example, think about such topics as marriage, parenting, singles, blended families, practice of spiritual disciplines, domestic violence, and financial well-being for families. Consider holding a planning retreat with the leaders you have identified. (See the Planning Retreat for Setting Ministries Strategies on the Guidelines CD.)

Plan the year ahead to address the needs of families in your congregation and in your community. Build a realistic budget to support what you plan for addressing these needs. With your leadership group, plan and schedule for such things as marriage enrichment classes, Christian Home Month, family retreat, divorce recovery courses, and parenting classes.

Carry out the plans you have made, enlisting the help of others in the congregation as needed to assist you and your leadership group. Remember to communicate frequently with the congregation (through newsletters, posters, e-mail, and other means) what is planned, how they can be involved, and the results of those plans.

Evaluate each plan you carry out as a group. Record recommendations for changes or improvements. The next person selected as leader in family ministries will be grateful for your records!

Use the additional resources listed on pages 31-32. These resources will provide more programming assistance, specific help in different areas of ministries, and study materials that can be used by small groups as they increase their understanding of family ministries.

Guidance for the Leader in Family Ministries

i t's not enough to say, "I will be in prayer as a leader of family ministries in my congregation." Setting a plan will help you keep in touch with God as you seek to lead the congregation.

Prayer and Spiritual Guidance

Recruit two or three persons in your congregation to be prayer partners for you. Ask each person to pray for you and your leadership in family ministries weekly. Ask each person to meet with you at least every three months throughout the year to pray as a group seeking God's guidance for you as a leader in family ministries.

Pray each week for specific families in your congregation. Depending on the size of your congregation, you may pray for only one family or for several. Ask for God's guidance for this family.

Read Scripture devotionally. As you go about your regular Scripture readings, consider adding this question to your reflections through the year: "What is this Scripture saying to me as a leader in family ministries and to our congregation regarding God's plan for our families?"

Use the prayer "Festival of the Christian Home" from *The United Methodist Book of Worship* (437) to guide your thoughts. Or, you may want to use the following prayer.

> *Gracious God, you guide us in every task. The task of caring for families seems very large. But you know the needs of each one, and you comfort and strengthen each family. May the light of your love shine upon those whose family members are in harmony with one another as well as those who are in discord. May you be with those families enjoying health as well as those families battling illness. May you strengthen families struggling to make ends meet as well as those with enough for their needs.*
>
> *We know that not every family is the same. Thank you for the love found in every family form. Thank you for the way you created people to care for and love one another as you care for and love us. Help us be aware that this is the gift of families. Help us confront cruelty and abuse, lifting up your vision of family as a place for support, love, and care. We pray today in the name of Jesus, our Savior. Amen.*

Knowing the Families We Seek to Serve

The work of family ministries involves promoting faith formation in families of many configurations. Take a moment and think about the variety of families in your congregation. You may have in one congregation:

- singles
- single-parent families
- families with children
- blended families (having children from previous marriages)
- married couples with no children
- grandparents raising grandchildren
- foster families
- widows and widowers

The Nurturing Community

The community provides the potential for nurturing human beings into the fullness of their humanity. We believe we have a responsibility to innovate, sponsor, and evaluate new forms of community that will encourage development of the fullest potential in individuals. Primary for us is the gospel understanding that all persons are important—because they are human beings created by God and loved through and by Jesus Christ and not because they have merited significance. We therefore support social climates in which human communities are maintained and strengthened for the sake of all persons and their growth....

A) The Family—We believe the family to be the basic human community through which persons are nurtured and sustained in mutual love, responsibility, respect, and fidelity. We affirm the importance of loving parents for all children. We also understand the family as encompassing a wider range of options than that of the two-generational unit of parents and children (the nuclear family). We affirm shared responsibility for parenting where there are two parents and encourage social, economic, and religious efforts to maintain and strengthen relationships within families in order that every member may be assisted toward complete personhood (*Book of Discipline*, ¶161A).

Families are in need of guidance and support to become centers of faith formation and to achieve a better quality of life in a physical, emotional, and spiritual sense. There is also a great concern of congregations to address the needs of families. A Christian family can provide the framework for faith formation for children, youth, and adults supporting one another to become disciples of Jesus Christ and to continue to walk with Christ in daily life. The church can respond by providing resources and leadership and by being an advocate for the needs of individual family members or the family unit. To discover these needs, survey the families of your congregation. Use or adapt this simple survey or the more detailed one. Both are on the Guidelines CD.

A Sample Family Ministries Survey (1)

The Family Ministries Team (or Council or Committee) wants to build its programs for families in accordance with the needs and interests of our families and our community. Please take a few minutes to respond to the following items. Your response is important to us. Return this to a member of our committee or leave it in the church office. Thank you!

1. Describe your family for us:

_____

_____

_____

2. Do you need resources for home devotions and worship?
    ____Yes____ No

Would you prefer these resources as ___ books ____church newsletter ____ articles ____ Web articles? (Check all that apply.)

3. What kinds of congregational activities would be important to you and your family? List your suggestions here:

_____

_____

_____

4. Tell us what topics or areas you would like to see our congregation provide information on regarding what's available in our community (for example, divorce recovery, financial planning, parenting).

_____

_____

_____

5. How family-friendly would you say our congregation is (very, so-so, poor, failing)?

_____

_____

_____

6. What could we do to improve?

_____

_____

_____

Advocate for Families

Depending on the organization of your church, plan to relate to the following church bodies:

Church Council: Your job would be to attend and report to regular meetings of the church council, keeping the council informed of the plans on behalf of families. Serve as an advocate for families, reminding the rest of the council of the needs of families as they relate to other areas of the church. For instance, when plans are made for the yearly stewardship campaign, remind those who are planning of the various types of families in your congregation and of the financial needs of families in your congregation that may affect the financial plan for the church.

Council on Family Ministries: This team may be recruited by the committee on nominations and lay leadership of the congregation. You may be responsible for recruiting your own team. In either case, you set up a meeting schedule, chair these meetings, and oversee the plans of this committee.

Ministry Team on Christian Education/Formation/Nurture Committee: In some congregations, the person in charge of family ministries is asked to serve on the nurture committee or the Christian education/formation committee. Attend meetings, help the committee plan with the needs of families in mind, and advocate for families.

Leading the Team

t he role of the family ministries team is to
Empower and provide resources for families so that they might:
- build faith traditions and rituals
- receive help in setting priorities (Christ at the center of the home, prayer, and devotional time)
- follow practices that allow them to walk with Christ in daily life and to grow in faith (with the support of the congregation)

Provide resources for families and for the congregation in life issues that are part of the home, the workplace, the church, and the community including:
- an up-to-date referral list of services in the congregation and in the community for families seeking financial help, help in abuse situations, marriage counseling, parenting help, mental and physical health needs
- regular study opportunities through the Sunday school or small groups to address ways to live faithfully in the family, as couples, as singles
- lending libraries of CDs, DVDs, videos, newsletters, and books that can be circulated among the families in the congregation

Serve as advocates for the needs of families of many configurations in the congregation and in the community.

Plan family ministries programs and opportunities, such as:
- January family ministries annual planning retreat
- May celebration of the Christian Home Month and Family Week
- church retreat
- workshops, small groups, and seminars that address needs of families

The Family Ministries Team Meetings

As you begin considering your leadership with the family ministries team, begin with prayer. God, who called you to this ministry, is also guiding you. It is in prayer that we listen to God's guidance and direction to lead us in ministry. Record biblical passages or ideas that you discover while in prayer.

_____

_____

_____

_____

_____

Think about those in the congregation who have been invited and feel led to work with you in family ministries. Pray for each person on the team. Call together those who have agreed to work on the team. Invite other leaders in the congregation who work with children, youth, and adult ministries to be part of the team.

Meet every month or two. You will need to increase the frequency when working on a major project. You may need to meet less frequently at other times of the year.

As you plan your meetings, consider using the following format.
1. Open with a prayer, including sharing known joys and concerns of families in the congregation (within privacy boundaries).
2. Include a devotional reading and a reflection on Scripture.
3. Review the role of the family ministry team. (Do this at every meeting. It's helpful to remind and renew commitment.)
4. Develop at the first meeting your vision and goals for the ministry of the team. Review these at subsequent meetings.
5. Design or review action plans.
6. Share reports as they relate to each goal.
7. Make assignments for work needed prior to the next meeting.
8. Make announcements.
9. Close with prayer.

Planning for Ministry

Set the vision. The mission of The United Methodist Church is *to make disciples for Jesus Christ for the transformation of the world.* To do this, the Church has a four-fold primary task for the local congregation: reaching out and receiving persons, relating them to God, nurturing them in the faith, and sending them out to make our communities more loving and just.

In order to accomplish this, what is your vision for your ministry area in your congregation?_____

Know those you seek to serve. The only way to know if you are serving those you seek to serve is to ASK THEM! Every leader needs to take time to survey the people, both with written polls and through informal conversation. In either case, remember: You are asking for their ideas, opinions, and desires. Your role is to record, to listen, and to clarify. You may use the survey on page 13 of this Guideline or the one on the CD. Keep the results before you as you set your goals.

Determine the results you seek. What are the expectations and goals that will be realized if you move toward your vision? Think in terms of what will be, not what you hope for. This is a subtle, but important difference. If you say, "We hope to increase the number of children and their families involved in the life of our church," there isn't much specific to go on. We name a result we are seeking: "Five more families actively involved in ministry from last year to the end of this year." Then name the strategies you will use to attract involvement of families. An example is: "Families in our church will receive and use devotional guides prepared by our team during the seasons of Advent and Lent." Next take the time to gather information on the number of families that did receive and use the guides. Keep these records and spread the word about the number of families whose lives have been impacted by this action. The "Guide to the Guidelines" on the CD includes important information on goal-setting. While the process here synopsizes this information, it will be helpful for you to go to that document for a fuller explanation.

To summarize what we find in the Guide to the Guidelines, we want to determine the results sought in family ministry within the congregational flow of ministry. The flow of ministry, described in ¶243 of the *2012 Book of Discipline* as the primary task, is summarized as

1) Reaching out to all people so that they may know the love of God
2) Nurturing them in the faith
3) Equipping them for ministry and
4) Sending them into the world to make the world more loving and just.

So setting goals within the categories of Reach-Nurture-Equip-Send is in keeping with the overall ministry of the congregation. Congregational goals are being set around the categories of:

• Disciples in Worship (worship attendance)
• Disciples Making New Disciples (number of professions of faith)
• Disciples Growing in Faith (number of small groups)
• Disciples Engaged in Mission (number of disciples doing outreach in the community and the world), and
• Disciples Sharing Their Resources for Mission (Giving for mission)

With each of these goals, the congregation then decides on the best strategies to use to increase the vitality of each area. Actions that are set using the SMART guidelines are more helpful than those that are vague. SMART actions are Specific, Measurable, Attainable, Relevant (to your purpose, mission, and ministry plan) and Time-framed. *The Planning Grid: Family Ministry* worksheet is on the Guidelines CD and at www.gbod.org/family.

Sample: From Result to Strategy

Result: Our congregation has 5 new families involved in regular participation by the end of this calendar year.
- Strategy: Plan weekly coffee and fellowship times beginning this January with specific individuals assigned to seek out and introduce new families to others in the congregation.
- Strategy: Make our church building more friendly to visitors by posting room location maps, color coding rooms for different age levels, and having enough greeters to take visitors to the location they need.
- Strategy: Welcome new visitors by taking gifts such as fresh-baked bread and cookies, along with an introductory video of our church within the first week of their visit.
- Strategy: Offer nursery and childcare for every event held by the congregation.

Result: Our congregation has two new small groups established by the end of this calendar year.
- Strategy: Establish a class for couples who have been married less than 5 years.
- Strategy: Recruit people to be part of a small group organized to study the issues of the community and how those issues are affecting families.
- Strategy: Create a small prayer group who meet and pray weekly for families who are experiencing illness and death of family members.
- Strategy: Hold a seminar during which families will plan for ways to recognize important family events through worship times at home.

Result: Involvement in mission and outreach increases by 10% from the previous year by the end of this calendar year.
- Strategy: In December, invite families to bring to the church mittens, scarves, and hats for distribution to the homeless in the community.
- Strategy: Prior to the start of school, offer opportunities for families to collect school supplies for use by children whose families can't afford to buy needed supplies.
- Strategy: Organize a Community Service Day and seek out places to serve that include children and youth as well as adults.

Recruit the team. For each event or activity planned, you will probably want leadership teams beyond your initial team. Achieving the results you seek may well depend on who is recruited for leadership. Think first, not of persons, but of traits. What traits in persons are needed for your leadership team? Now, who are the persons in your congregation or your community who possess those traits?

You may be thinking: *This is easy enough for a small congregation, but we have 1200 members!"* On the other hand, leaders in small congregations are thinking: *"Just where are the people we need going to come from?"* In smaller congregations, think of those doing something similar already. Can you ask them to expand what they're doing to encompass something new? In larger congregations, identify staff or key leaders who can help you know who might have the traits you seek. Sometimes a simple announcement in worship or through the newsletter of the traits you are seeking will bring forth volunteers you might not have considered.

List here the "ideal" leadership team for each of your goals.

_____

_____

_____

_____

_____

_____

_____

_____

Approach those you are asking with a clear plan of what you are seeking to do and how you see them contributing to the team to achieve the goals.

See the "Planning Retreat for Setting Ministry Strategies" on the Guidelines CD.

Put plans into action. Moving from plans to actual happenings is the sticking point for many congregations. One helpful way to begin to see what your plans might look like is to set deadlines for when certain things are to be accomplished. Use the suggested annual planning calendar found on page 28 of this Guideline. As you move your plans into action, be specific about who will be responsible for each step of the plan; the outside leadership needed; the budget needed to fulfill the plan; the materials needed for each step of the plan; and securing places for specific programs, courses, or events. In addition to your general plans and strategies, there are some particular resources or categories of ministry to keep in mind.

CHRISTIAN HOME MONTH

At the 2012 General Conference, delegates amended and readopted the resolution naming May as Christian Home Month. This resolution encourages congregations to emphasize family worship in the home, worship and program planning in the congregation, and prayer on behalf of families. The Office of Family Ministries of the General Board of Discipleship produces annual resources to be used for observing Christian Home Month. The themes for 2013-2016 are as follows: 2013: Families Called to Love; 2014: Families Called to Peace; 2015: Families Called to Justice; 2016 Families Called to Hope. The resources are available online at www.gbod.org/family or in print from the Office of Family Ministries, General Board of Discipleship, P.O. Box 340003, Nashville, TN 37202-0003.

INTERGENERATIONAL MINISTRIES

Intergenerational ministries at church can offer opportunities for children, youth, and adults to learn and be in fellowship together. In church while most of the learning opportunities are specific to an age group, these multi-generational or cross-generational times can show how all of us as children of God learn from one another regardless of age. Some churches use the following for intergenerational experiences: workshops for Advent or Lent, all-church Sunday school, Church heritage studies, mission projects, church retreats. The resource list in this Guideline and the GBOD website provide resources for intergenerational learning and fellowship.

MARRIAGE ENRICHMENT IN THE CONGREGATION

Congregational support of marriages is key to family ministry. In planning for congregational support of marriages, examine what you are currently doing to support marriages actively in your congregation and in your community. Use the following areas to analyze where you need to establish programs or resources for your congregation.

Premarriage support. This would include youth classes on marriage and commitment, premarital counseling with clergy for couples planning marriage, mentoring programs to pair couples anticipating marriage with married couples for advice and support. The official United Methodist guide for pre-marriage counseling is *Growing Love in Christian Marriage* (see Resources).

Ongoing marriage support. Plans here would include regular studies for married couples through Sunday school classes or small groups; yearly marriage enrichment retreats provided by the congregation or cooperatively with other congregations in the community or area; and mentoring programs to pair couples with other couples for advice and support. Consider joining an organization that trains leaders in couple communication, such as Marriage Encounter/Engaged Encounter United Methodist; the Association for Couples in Marriage Enrichment; and Marriage Enrichment, Inc. Further information on these organizations is available from the Family Ministry Office, the General Board of Discipleship (1-877-899-2780, ext. 7170).

Community information and referral services. Plans would include up-to-date information on support and counseling for couples available in the community, including financial planning, domestic violence, extended family issues, Twelve-Step programs, and Christian counseling services.

Crisis intervention. While a single congregation may not be able to provide the crisis intervention in marriages where there have been deep hurts, the congregation can research and identify community resources for this area. The book *Forgiving Your Family* (see Resources) contains helpful information for individual or small group studies around what is needed when deep hurt occurs.

CLERGY FAMILIES

As you work on addressing the needs of families in your congregation and in your community don't forget the needs of your clergy family. The phrase "life in the fishbowl" is often used to describe how a clergy family feels it lives. There are pressures felt by both the clergy spouse and by children in the household. Providing ways for clergy to establish time for their own families may be part of the support you provide. Work with the chairperson of the pastor/parish relations committee on ways to best address the needs of clergy families.

CREATING SAFE SANCTUARIES®

As much as we would like for every family to be a family of love, peace, and justice, this isn't so. Many people experience within the family physical, mental, emotional, or sexual abuse. Those whom they trust and love the most become those who hurt them on a regular basis. The church is called to be the safe sanctuary for family members caught in the cycle of violence and abuse. Consider these words from the *Discipline*:

Family Violence and Abuse—We recognize that family violence and abuse in all its forms—verbal, psychological, physical, sexual—is detrimental to the covenant of the human community. We encourage the Church to provide a safe environment, counsel, and support for the victim. While we deplore the actions of the abuser, we affirm that person to be in need of God's redeeming love (¶161G).

Advocate in your congregation for:
- Sermons, prayers, workshops, lectures, Sunday school classes that address the presence of violence in families.
- Published information distributed through newsletters, display racks, and on the church's website giving the indicators of abuse. Include what signs to look for, not just with children but also with youth and adults.
- Clear policies and forms related to the recruiting, screening, and hiring of those who work in the church.
- Creating a congregational plan for responding to allegations of abuse if they occur in the church.

For more help in this area, purchase the *Safe Sanctuaries®* books (see Resources). These and other resources can serve as a guide for planning a congregational response to abuse.

Evaluation of Family Ministries

Written and verbal evaluations help us (1) plan for improvements when we repeat specific programs, (2) provide information to those who follow us as leaders, and (3) identify future directions. Following each specific program you implement, ask participants, planners, and leaders to complete an evaluation form. You may use the following or develop your own. In each of the columns, define your terms. For example, the congregation will
- Reach—more families yearly
- Nurture—increase family involvement in worship, both at church and in the home
- Equip—increase small group opportunities for families together and for individual family members
- Send—provide mission and service experiences for families

Planning Grid: Family Ministries

Disciples:	Reach	Nurture	Equip	Send
Worship	Strategy:	Strategy:	Strategy:	Strategy:
Make New Disciples	Strategy:	Strategy:	Strategy:	Strategy:
Engage in Growing as a Disciple	Strategy:	Strategy:	Strategy:	Strategy:
Engage in Mission	Strategy:	Strategy:	Strategy:	Strategy:
Give to Mission	Strategy:	Strategy:	Strategy:	Strategy:

There is a Sample Evaluation form on the Guidelines CD that asks participants about the best part of the event, what could be improved, what led them to participate, how they found out about it, and what else they might need.

What Results Do You Want?

Good evaluation depends on having in mind the ends, results, or goals that you desire. If you have not thought ahead to what you want to accomplish, your evaluation may center only on numbers—how many people attended how many events—rather than what is happening in the lives of the people you serve. While you want your ministry to reach people, the ultimate goal is to make disciples of Jesus Christ for the transformation of the world. That means you need to see people-oriented results: the changes in people's lives that indicate a growing, deepening faith that leads to significant discipleship.

The "Guide to the Guidelines" on the CD, and a similar document, "Measures Evaluation Tool," found at www.umvitalcongregations.com in the "Setting Goals" tab, can be of great assistance in planning, goal setting, and evaluating.

As you complete the planning grid above (or one of your choosing) keep in mind what impact you desire for each of those strategies and the specific ways you will know if you are achieving those results. This will include quantitative things (what you can count, like attendance or giving or hours expended) and qualitative things (like changed behaviors, new spiritual practices, and altered attitudes and values).

Following each event, class, group, or experience offered by your ministry team, plan for an evaluation time at your first meeting afterwards. Invite the pastor or other church leaders to participate. Use the following statements to guide your discussion.

1. Our goal for this program was to . . .

2. The results we expected were . . .

3. The results we achieved were . . .

4. Ways we would improve are to . . .

5. What we need to do next is to . . .

Family Ministry Models

f amily ministry" recognizes that families come in many shapes and sizes. Family units may include several persons who are not actually related biologically, persons who have created family for whatever reason, families with no children, families in which the parenting role is filled by a different relative, or other configuration.

A Flexible "Family" Concept

Such a wide divergence requires creativity and flexibility in planning for families in their many forms. Consider these ideas and suggestions in your ministry strategies.

PROVIDING ONGOING PARENTING AND GRANDPARENTING CLASSES

- Focusing on God: How to parent so that you encourage faith formation of your children.
- Communication in the Family: Differences in communicating with children and youth.
- Family Conferencing: Format and topics for practicing Christian conferencing in the home and making decisions together as a family.
- Sexuality: Knowing the stages of sexuality and ways to foster healthy sexuality.
- Prayer: Ways to pray and to establish routines of prayer in the home.
- Discipline: Ways to appropriately discipline children at various ages.
- Media: Messages in media and ways to recognize media influence on children and youth. Safety in the area of technology is a particular need.
- Drug and Alcohol Abuse: Signs of abuse; what to do when abuse occurs.

CREATING CATEGORIES OF FAMILY MINISTRY RELATED TO FAMILY TYPES

Some ministry plans will address the needs of all families in a congregation. However, you may want to plan with the following general family types in mind. (These are illustrative—not exhaustive—related to type):

- Singles. Yes, singles are a part of family ministry. Indeed, many adult members of a congregation have always been single or have been "singled" through divorce, death, or loss of a significant relationship.
- Families with Children in the Home. No matter if a family involves one, two, or more adults, if rearing children is part of the mix, then these adults will have many of the same needs and issues.
- Adult Children, Aging Parents. This would include addressing

care-giving needs related to sharing a household with older adults, as well as adult children who live in another location than their parents but have responsibilities related to care.
- Family Members who have Special Care Needs. Families with children, youth, or adults who have constant medical or safety needs may often feel isolated and even unwelcome in a congregation. Addressing issues of hospitality and care can be part of what shapes this ministry area.

MAKING MILESTONES MINISTRIES THE FOCUS OF FAMILY MINISTRIES

Milestones are those important times in the lives of individuals and families through the life span. Family ministry shaped around milestones includes home celebrations, worship acknowledgement of events, and outreach opportunities at times of both celebration and pain. Some important milestones to consider include:
- Births and Adoptions
- Start of School
- Beginning a first job or new job
- Graduations
- Receiving a Driver's License
- Establishing a Home or Closing the "Family Homestead"
- Marriage
- Divorce
- Death of a Family Member
- Moving or other transitions

PROVIDING SUPPORT FOR FAMILIES FOR SHAPING DEVOTIONAL LIFE BY THE CHRISTIAN YEAR

The Christian year shapes the worshipping life of a congregation. Providing resources and experiences for home reflection, ritual, and devotion strengthens the home as a place nurture and mission.
- Overview of the Seasons of the Christian Year provided in the newsletter, on the church website, or as a special small group study.
- Advent/Christmas/Epiphany workshops for learning about the season, making such items as an Advent Wreath for home use and writing prayers.
- Lenten studies that help family members focus more deeply on spiritual practices.
- Easter celebrations for the home that include hymns, Scripture, and prayer.
- Pentecost observances, including decorating both home and church with red banners.

ADVOCATING FOR HOUSEHOLDS TO ADOPT A "FAMILY NIGHT IN"

Family Night In is the practice of a family to stay home together one night a week for a time for devotions, conversation, fun, and games.

- Determine a day of the week that works most weeks for the family. (Be flexible. Some weeks there will be no day that works well.)
- Establish a schedule for what you want to happen during your family night in. A common format is dinner together (either prepared in the home or purchased but eating together at home); games, movies, or activities together; devotions and prayer.
- Family Meal: Rotate responsibilities of different family members for preparing the meal. Have once-a-month meals where a family member gets to choose his or her favorite food for the meal. Try new foods. Once a month have a "theme" meal where new foods will be tried by all.
- Family Fun: This can include family viewing movies together; looking through old photo albums and remembering family stories; taking time to write to family members who are not living in the home; playing board games together; interviewing one another about topics that are currently in the news.
- Family Devotions: Include a prayer circle with everyone taking turns to pray. Read Bible stories and share the meaning of the story and how it relates to your family.
- Family Covenant: Make a Prayer-Love-Share covenant. Include ways members of the family want to pray together, love one another, and share with others in need.

Calendar for Family Ministries

JANUARY

- Form a small group or team to serve as the family life council or family ministries team to plan for family ministries in your congregation.
- Order family ministries resources from Cokesbury and the General Board of Discipleship.
- Plan to celebrate the seasons of the Christian year with families (Lent, Holy Week, Easter, Pentecost, Advent, Christmas, and Epiphany) by providing special programs, worship, workshops, seminars, groups, and forums.
- Observe the Baptism of the Lord through a renewal of baptism and classes or workshops on baptism.

FEBRUARY

- Participate in the celebration of African American Families Month.
- Celebrate marriages. Recognize milestones of couples in the congregation.
- Involve families in the planning of Vacation Bible School with classes for all ages.
- Plan a one-day Lenten retreat for families focusing on prayer and Bible study.
- Invite community leaders who work with families to lead a seminar. Provide nursery and childcare for younger children.

MARCH

- Order the Christian Home Month booklet from the Office of Family Ministries at the General Board of Discipleship.
- Begin plans for celebrating Christian Home month, including a worship service in the month of May.
- Involve families in experiences of sharing and service with needy families in the community.
- Provide an intergenerational workshop on prayer.
- Conduct a series of classes on single parenting and step-parenting.
- Review plans for Family Ministries for the remainder of the year.

APRIL

- Involve families in sharing time and service with needy families in the community.
- Offer a series of seminars on couples enrichment and relationship building.
- Observe Earth Day. Publish in the church newsletter suggestions for families to observe Earth Day in the home.

MAY

- Celebrate Christian Home Month with a worship service and a fellowship meal.
- Involve families in sharing time and service with needy families in the community.
- Meet with the family team to evaluate the worship, programs, and activities of Christian Home Month. Ask questions such as: What went well? What needs improvement? What impact did this have on participants? (How do we know?)
- Encourage families to participate in vacation Bible school.

JUNE

- Involve families in sharing time and service with needy families in the community.
- Design and distribute a prayer card that families can use while on vacation.
- Plan a Church Family Picnic or Family Retreat for families of many configurations, including a devotional, prayers, and praise.
- Involve families in service projects in the community.
- Put together a devotional guide for families to take on vacation.

JULY

- Offer intergenerational programs on a Friday night at the church, with a potluck dinner and games for all ages.
- Encourage families to visit a neighbor.
- Invite families to a lock-in (spend the night) at the church with devotions, family prayers, games, and fellowship.

AUGUST

- Provide a back-to-school devotional for children and their families.
- Work with your school system to provide backpacks for children in families who cannot afford school supplies.
- Design short-term Bible study time for youth and their families.
- Plan to celebrate Children's Sabbath in October.

SEPTEMBER

- Begin a small-group study with families on a topic of concern in your community.
- Conduct parenting and grandparenting classes using the book *Parents and Grandparents as Spiritual Guides* (see Resources).
- Publish a listing of community resources that support couples.

OCTOBER

- Attend the World Communion Sunday service as a family.
- Plan and lead the congregation in a great day of caring with service opportunities for families in the community.
- Celebrate the Children's Sabbath with a service to remember children and their families.
- Option: Celebrate Christian Home Month with a worship service in this month.

NOVEMBER

- Provide devotional resources for families to celebrate Thanksgiving at home.
- Ask a group of families to develop an Advent prayer calendar for different families.
- Offer families opportunities to serve in soup kitchens or homeless shelters (perhaps throughout the winter).

DECEMBER

- Plan a one-day Advent retreat for families.
- Encourage families to celebrate Advent at home with an Advent wreath and a family devotional every Sunday.
- Invite families to write stories about the nativity sets they use in their homes. Publish these in the church newsletter.
- Offer an evening prayer service on New Year's Eve for families.

Resources

**Denotes our top picks

- *Baptism: Understanding God's Gift*, by Edward Phillips and Sara Webb Phillips (Nashville: Discipleship Resources, 2012. ISBN 978-0-88177-599-0). Available from www.amazon.com.

- *Birthed in Prayer: Pregnancy as a Spiritual Journey*, by Kim Barker, Linda de Meillon, Leigh Harrison (Nashville: Upper Room Books, 2008. ISBN 978-0-8358-9941-3). Includes real-life stories and encouragement.

- *Breaking and Mending: Divorce and God's Grace*, by Mary Lou Redding (Nashville: Upper Room Books, 1998. ISBN 978-0-8358-0855-2). Looks at the spiritual issues and struggles that accompany a divorce.

- *The Children's Minister*, by Rita B. Hays (Nashville: Discipleship Resources, 2008. ISBN 978-0-88177-527-3). Includes help for ministering with families of children at milestones and in times of crisis.

- **Christian Home Month Manual*. Office of Family Ministries, the General Board of Discipleship (1-877-899-2780, Ext. 7170). Free yearly manual for celebrating Christian Home Month in May or another month.

- *Church Programs & Celebrations for All Generations*, by Rachel Gilmore (Valley Forge: Judson Press, 2010. ISBN 978-0-8170-1642-5). Activities for seasonal worship and holiday celebrations.

- *Credo: Confirmation Guide for Parents, Mentors, and Adult Leaders*, by MaryJane Pierce Norton (Nashville: Cokesbury, 2010. ISBN-13: 978-1-426-70627-1). Suggests ways parents and adults can learn alongside confirmation youth and extend the learning into the home.

- **CyberSafety for Families* CD, by Paul O'Briant (Nashville: Discipleship Resources, 2010. ISBN 978-0-88177-592-1). Training-kit on CD with teaching plans, handouts, and slide presentations for teaching parents and other adults about ways to keep children and teens safe online.

- **Family: The Forming Center, Revised Edition*, by Marjorie Thompson (Nashville: Upper Room Books, 1997. ISBN 978-0-8358-0798-2). Suggests models, rituals, and celebrations for a Christ-centered home.

- *Forgiving Your Family: A Journey to Healing*, by Kathleen Fischer (Nashville: Upper Room Books, 2005. ISBN 978-0-8358-9802-7). Real-life stories of hurt and healing within families.

- *Gen2Gen: Sharing Jesus Across the Generations*, ed. Richard H. Gentzler, Jr., Melanie C. Gordon, Craig Kennet Miller, Abby Parker

(Nashville: Discipleship Resources, 2012. ISBN 978-0-47000-197.1).
Available from www.amazon.com.

- *Growing Love in Christian Marriage: Pastor's Manual, Revised*, by Jane and Clifton Ives (Nashville: Abingdon Press, 2001. ISBN 978-0-687-07604-8). *Couple's Manual,* by Joan and Richard Hunt (ISBN 978-1-687-08221-8). Material for pre-wedding counseling sessions for both clergy and couples.

- *In Love Again & Making It Work: Successful Remarriage*, by Dick Dunn (Nashville: Discipleship Resources, 2008. ISBN 978-0-88177-534-1).

- *Life in the Fish Bowl: Everyday Challenges of Pastors and Their Families*, by F. Belton Joyner Jr. (Nashville: Abingdon Press, 2006. ISBN 978-0-687-33294-6).

- *Making Love Last a Lifetime: Biblical Perspectives on Love, Marriage, and Sex*, by Adam Hamilton (Nashville: Abingdon Press, 2004). With a Pastor's Guide; Leader's Guide; Participant's Book; VHS Tape and DVD.

- *Parents and Grandparents as Spiritual Guides: Nurturing Children of the Promise*, by Betty Shannon Cloyd (Nashville: Upper Room Books, 2000. ISBN 978-0-8358-0923-8). Explores the ways parents and grandparents can introduce children to God.

- *Safe Sanctuaries: The Church Responds to Abuse, Neglect, and Exploitation of Older Adults*, by Joy Thornburg Melton (Nashville: Discipleship Resources, 2012. ISBN 978-0-88177-613-3).

- *Safe Sanctuaries: Reducing the Risk of Abuse in the Church for Children and Youth*, by Joy Thornton Melton (Nashville: Discipleship Resources, 2008. ISBN 978-0-88177-543-3). *Safe Sanctuaries for Ministers: Best Practices and Ethical Decisions,* by Joy Thornton Melton (Nashville: Discipleship Resources, 2009. ISBN 978-0-88177-560-0).

AGENCY CONTACTS

- www.gbod.org/family. Prayers, devotions, suggestions for celebrating holidays and holy days in the home.

- www.gcsrw.org. Study on clergy spouses and families, as well as resources for caring for clergy families.

- www.umc-gbcs.org. Societal issues and families.

- www.ncccusa.org. Suggestions and bibliographies for family ministry.

- www.vitalcongregations.com. Helps for measuring, planning, evaluating, and complying with the conference assessments on vitality in your church.